KING ARTHUR
and his KNIGHTS

Told by George Gibson

Editors: Rebecca Raynes, Monika Marszewska
Design and art direction: Nadia Maestri
Computer graphics: Simona Corniola
Illustrations: Giovanni Manna
Picture research: Laura Lagomarsino

© 2003 Black Cat

DEALINK, DEAFLIX are trademarks licensed by De Agostini SpA

Picture credits
The Royal Photographic Society Collection, Bath: 4; Lambeth Palace Library, London, UK/Bridgeman Art Library: 9; By permission of the British Library: 26, 51; Musée Condé, Chantilly, France/Bridgeman Art Library: 53; Reproduced by kind permission of Hampshire County Council: 74.

All rights reserved. No part of this book may be reproduced, stored in a retrieval system, or transmitted, in any form or by any means, electronic, mechanical, photocopying, recording or otherwise, without the written permission of the publisher.

We would be happy to receive your comments
and suggestions, and give you any other
information concerning our material.
Our e-mail and web-site addresses are:
info@blackcat-cideb.com
blackcat-cideb.com

Printed in Italy by Italgrafica, Novara

CONTENTS

CHAPTER ONE	Young Arthur	10
CHAPTER TWO	The Sword in the Stone	15
CHAPTER THREE	Britain has a King	20
CHAPTER FOUR	Excalibur	29
CHAPTER FIVE	Arthur meets Guinevere	33
CHAPTER SIX	The Five Kings	40
CHAPTER SEVEN	Lancelot	45
CHAPTER EIGHT	The Holy Grail	58
CHAPTER NINE	King Arthur goes to Avalon	65

Dossiers

Was King Arthur only a Legend?	4
Before Arthur's Time	7
Knights	26
Castles	51
Old Castles of Great Interest	54
The Round Table	74
Where was King Arthur Buried?	76

UNDERSTANDING THE TEXT 13, 18, 23, 32, 36, 43, 48, 61, 70

Special Features:

PET	PET-style exercises	13, 14, 18, 23, 25, 32, 36, 39, 43, 48, 57, 61, 62, 63, 64, 70, 78
T: GRADES 4, 5	Trinity-style exercises	19, 44, 63

PROJECT ON THE WEB	57
Exit Test	78
Key to the Exit Test	80

Was King Arthur only a Legend?

No, King Arthur was not only a legend. In the ninth century, a historian called Nennius wrote a book called *Historia Britonum*. It was a history of Britain, about the life of the Celtic leader,[1] Arthur, and his knights.[2]

Nennius wrote that Arthur was a great Celtic military leader of the 5th and 6th century. He fought against the Saxons from the year 513 to 537. He and his men won many battles against the Saxons.

His people loved and remembered him for centuries after. There are lots of old ballads, songs, poems and stories about Arthur and his knights.

In 1470, Sir Thomas Malory wrote about King Arthur and his castle, Camelot. His writings are a complete and accurate record[3] of the King's life and times.

Arthur's army confronting the Saxons from Jean Wauquelin's Chronicle (15th century).

1. **leader** : commander, ruler.
2. **knights** : ['naitz]
3. **record** : a writing about events and happenings.

Today there are many books and films in different languages on this exciting subject. King Arthur is so famous that he is part of the Breton literary cycle.

Important Places During Arthur's Time

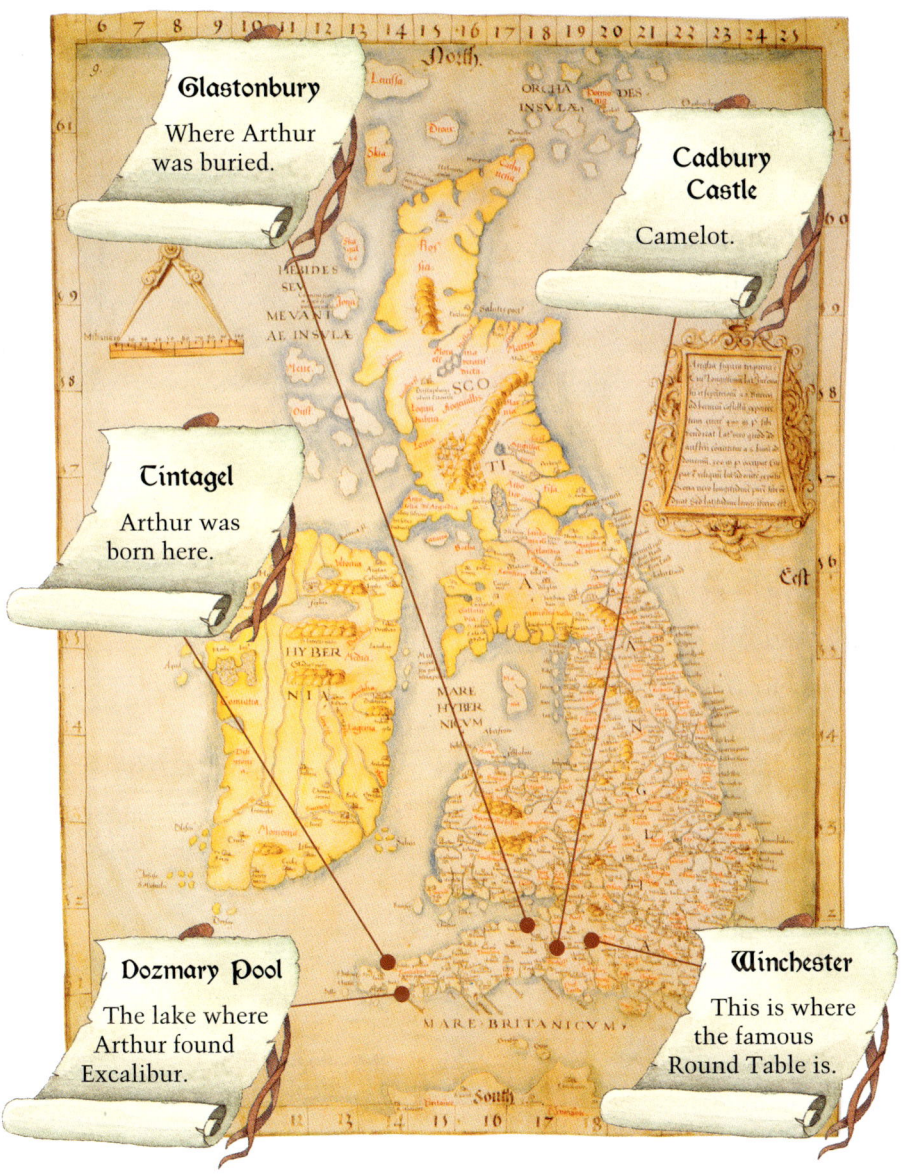

Glastonbury
Where Arthur was buried.

Cadbury Castle
Camelot.

Tintagel
Arthur was born here.

Dozmary Pool
The lake where Arthur found Excalibur.

Winchester
This is where the famous Round Table is.

1 Match the correct parts of the sentences.

a. Nennius was ☐
b. Nennius wrote that King Arthur ☐
c. From the year 513 to 537 ☐
d. His people remembered him ☐
e. *Historia Britonum* ☐

1. with songs, poems and stories.
2. is a historic book about King Arthur and his times.
3. was a great Celtic leader of the 6th century.
4. Arthur fought against the Saxons.
5. a historian of the 9th century.

2 Look at the map on page 5 and answer the following questions.

a. Where was Arthur born?
   ....

b. Where is the Round Table?
   ....

c. What is the name of the lake where Arthur found Excalibur?
   ....

d. Where was Camelot?
   ....

e. Where was Arthur buried?
   ....

Before Arthur's Time

The first inhabitants of Britain were probably the Celts. They came from Germany in the third century BC.

The Roman general, Julius Caesar, invaded Britain in the year 54 BC. He had 25,000 soldiers and 2,000 horses. But he did not stay in Britain. He went to fight the Gauls in France.

In 43 AD. the Roman Emperor Claudius invaded Britain. This time the Romans stayed. Britain became a Roman province called Britannia.

The Romans built roads, walls and towns. There are many Roman remains[1] in Britain. Hadrian's Wall is a good example. It was built by the Roman Emperor Hadrian in 122 AD. He built it in the north of Britain to keep out the Scots. It is about 120 kilometres long. It took six years to build.

The Romans left Britain in 410 AD. after 350 years.

During the fifth and sixth century, the Angles and the Saxons invaded Britain. The legendary King Arthur fought against these invaders and others.

These are two sides of a Roman coin. It was made to celebrate Claudius's victory in Britain. One side shows Emperor Claudius and the other shows him riding his horse. Notice the writing 'De Britann' on the coin.

1. **remains** : (here) parts of old buildings which are left.

Can you find the names of three Roman Emperors and the name of the Roman province? Circle them.

S	X	O	F	G	J	Z	V	R	A	O
D	S	H	A	D	R	I	A	N	G	H
B	S	R	Q	Y	P	E	D	I	H	Z
R	Z	O	J	C	A	E	S	A	R	L
I	O	X	R	L	V	R	G	Q	K	W
T	R	G	D	A	M	T	H	M	E	O
A	B	L	I	U	G	V	S	I	J	D
N	P	C	N	D	S	U	O	W	L	X
N	V	J	B	I	W	F	A	G	P	J
I	O	H	F	U	Q	P	F	B	V	C
A	U	K	I	S	E	O	P	E	R	K

Write a sentence about a Roman Emperor.

....
....
....
....

Write a sentence about the Roman province.

....
....
....
....

BEFORE YOU READ

What is a legend?

A legend begins as a true story, but as the years pass some things are added to it, and some things are forgotten.

So, a legend is a mix of historical facts and popular fantasy.

 The story of King Arthur is a very popular legend.
This is a picture of King Arthur when he became King.

The crowning of King Arthur from St. Alban's Chronicle (late 15th century).

What is your favourite legend?

....

CHAPTER ONE

Young Arthur

 In the year 493, Uther Pendragon became King of Britain. He had a counsellor named Merlin. Merlin was also a magician.[1]

When King Uther's son Arthur was born, Merlin said, 'Your son must grow up away from the court. It is safer!'

Merlin gave the baby son to Sir Ector and his wife. They raised[2] him well.

When King Uther died in 509, Britain had no king. The country had many problems.

---

1. **magician** : person who can make strange things happen by magic.
2. **raised** : looked after, brought up.

 # King Arthur and his Knights

Merlin went to the Archbishop of Canterbury [1] and said, 'Britain must have a king. We must find one. Call all the noblemen of the kingdom. Tell them to meet at the great church in London on Christmas Day. There, God will show us the new king.'

On Christmas Day, all the noblemen were in the great church. Outside the church there was a big stone with a sword in it. These words were written on the big stone:

> He who pulls the sword
> out of this stone
> is the true King of Britain.

---

1. **Archbishop of Canterbury** : important religious leader in Canterbury.

UNDERSTANDING THE TEXT

 Read the questions below.
For each question, choose the correct answer – A, B, C or D.

1. What happened in the year 493?
   - **A** ☐ Sir Ector died.
   - **B** ☐ Merlin was born.
   - **C** ☐ Uther Pendragon became King of Britain.
   - **D** ☐ King Arthur was born.

2. Who was Merlin the magician?
   - **A** ☐ King Uther's counsellor.
   - **B** ☐ King Uther's father.
   - **C** ☐ The Archbishop of Canterbury.
   - **D** ☐ Sir Ector's brother.

3. Why did Merlin gave King Uther's baby son to Sir Ector and his wife?
   - **A** ☐ Because they lived in King Uther's castle.
   - **B** ☐ Because it was safer for the baby to grow up away from the court.
   - **C** ☐ Because they paid Merlin for the baby.
   - **D** ☐ Because King Uther did not want the baby.

4. What happened in the year 509?
   - **A** ☐ Merlin became the King's counsellor.
   - **B** ☐ King Uther died.
   - **C** ☐ Arthur was born.
   - **D** ☐ The Archbishop of Canterbury died.

5. What did Merlin say to the Archbishop of Canterbury?
   - **A** ☐ 'God will show us the new king on Christmas Day.'
   - **B** ☐ 'A nobleman of London will be the new king.'
   - **C** ☐ 'You must be the new king.'
   - **D** ☐ 'Sir Ector will be the new king.'

6. What was written on the stone?
   - **A** ☐ 'He who breaks this sword is the true King of Britain.'
   - **B** ☐ 'No one must pull this sword out of the stone.'
   - **C** ☐ 'He who pulls the sword out of this stone is the true King of Britain.'
   - **D** ☐ 'He who pulls the sword out of this stone is the new Archbishop of Canterbury.'

BEFORE YOU READ

PET

1 Listen to Chapter Two.
For each question, put a tick (✓) in the correct box.

1. Who tried to pull the sword out of the stone?
   - A ☐ Sir Ector.
   - B ☐ The noblemen.
   - C ☐ Merlin.

2. Where was the sword on New Year's Day?
   - A ☐ In the stone.
   - B ☐ In the castle.
   - C ☐ In the church.

3. Who pulled the sword out of the stone?
   - A ☐ The Archbishop of Canterbury.
   - B ☐ Sir Ector.
   - C ☐ Arthur.

4. What did Sir Ector tell Arthur?
   - A ☐ 'I'm not your real father.'
   - B ☐ 'I'm the King of Britain.'
   - C ☐ 'I'm your father.'

5. Who raised Arthur like a son?
   - A ☐ Merlin.
   - B ☐ Sir Ector.
   - C ☐ The Archbishop of Canterbury.

6. What must Arthur do now?
   - A ☐ He must give the sword to the Archbishop.
   - B ☐ He must leave Britain.
   - C ☐ He must go and do his duty.

CHAPTER TWO

THE SWORD IN THE STONE

ach nobleman tried to pull the sword out of the stone. No one was able to do it.
On New Year's Day, the sword was still in the stone. Arthur was there with Sir Ector.

Arthur pulled the sword out of the stone without difficulty! This was the sign from God. All the noblemen were surprised. He was the new King of Britain.

Sir Ector said, 'Arthur, you are now the King of Britain.'

Arthur said, 'Father, I don't want to leave you!'

King Arthur
and his Knights

Sir Ector said, 'I'm not your real father. I don't know who you are. The magician Merlin brought you to us when you were born. I raised you like a son, and I love you. Now you are a king. God wants you to lead [1] Britain. You must go and do your duty.' [2]

Merlin said to the noblemen, 'This is King Uther's son and he is our new king!'

Young Arthur first became a knight. Then he became King of Britain.

1. **lead** : govern.
2. **do your duty** : accept your responsibilities.

UNDERSTANDING THE TEXT

PET

1 Look at the statements below about Chapter Two.
Decide if each statement is correct or incorrect.
If it is correct, tick (✓) A.
If it is not correct, tick (✓) B.

	A	B
1. No nobleman was able to pull the sword out of the stone.	☐	☐
2. Arthur was in London with Merlin.	☐	☐
3. Arthur pulled the sword out of the stone easily.	☐	☐
4. All the noblemen were angry.	☐	☐
5. Arthur did not want to leave Sir Ector.	☐	☐
6. Sir Ector was not Arthur's real father.	☐	☐
7. Merlin said, 'This is Sir Ector's son and he is our new king!'	☐	☐
8. First Arthur was a knight, then he became King.	☐	☐

2 Match the words below with their opposites.

a. first
b. pull
c. difficult
d. true
e. new
f. born
g. big
h. bring
i. love
j. go

1. come
2. old
3. small
4. take
5. hate
6. push
7. false
8. easy
9. die
10. last

3. Demonstrative pronouns

In Chapter Two, we saw this sentence:

This was the sign from God.

The demonstrative pronouns are: *this, that, these* and *those*.
This and *these* refer to things close to you. *That* and *those* refer to things farther away.

Complete the sentences below with a suitable demonstrative pronoun.

a. Today is Christmas Day, and all the noblemen are in the church.
   .... is an important day.
b. 'Who is the old man at the back of the church?' asked Arthur.
   '............... is the Archbishop of Canterbury,' said Sir Ector.
c. 'Look at the young boy here with the sword,' said Merlin.
   '............... is the new King of Britain.'
d. Many men are in front of the church over there.
   .... are the noblemen of Britain.
e. .... are the words written on the stone in front of the church.
f. Sir Ector was outside the church.
   '............... is the great church of London,' he said.

T: GRADE 4

4. Topic – Places

The sword in the stone was outside a great church in London.

Bring to the class a photo/map/souvenir of London or a city you like. Talk to the class about this city. Use the following questions to help you.

a. Describe this city. Where is it? What is it like? Is it big or small?
b. What can you visit in this city? What are the most interesting things to see? Where are the best places to go for a person of your age?
c. When are you going to visit this city again?

CHAPTER THREE

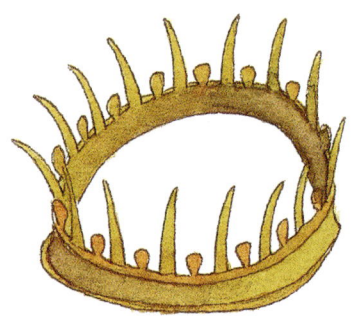

BRITAIN HAS A KING

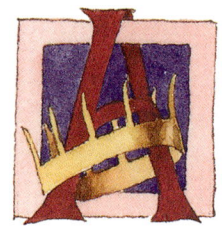

Arthur was a young king. He was about twenty years old. He lived at Camelot. His first years as king were difficult. He fought against many enemies from other lands, particularly the Saxons. Some noblemen of his court caused trouble.[1] They did not want to obey[2] a young king.

King Arthur was very adventurous. He liked riding his horse and looking for adventures. He was courageous, loyal and friendly. His people loved him.

One day, King Arthur was riding in the forest. He saw a fountain. Near the fountain there was a knight named Sir Pellinore.

1. **trouble** : problems.
2. **obey** : follow, take orders from.

KING ARTHUR
and his KNIGHTS

'Stop!' said Sir Pellinore. 'You cannot go past the fountain! You must fight with me first!'

King Arthur answered, 'I'm ready to fight!' The two knights began fighting. First they fought with their lances.[1] Then they fought with their swords.

During the fight, Arthur's sword broke. Sir Pellinore said, 'I'm the winner!'

At that moment, Merlin appeared and said, 'Pellinore, this knight is your king! King Arthur!'

Sir Pellinore stopped fighting immediately.

1. **lances** :

UNDERSTANDING THE TEXT

PET

Read the text below and choose the correct word for each space. For each question, mark the letter next to the correct word – A, B, C or D.

Young King Arthur lived (0) ..A...... Camelot. He fought (1) .... the Saxons and (2) .... enemies. Some of Arthur's noblemen did not want to (3) .... him. Young Arthur liked looking (4) .... adventures. He was (5) .... in the forest (6) .... day and he saw (7) .... fountain. A knight called Sir Pellinore said, 'Do not go past that fountain. Fight with me first!'

The two men began fighting with (8) .... lances and swords. Arthur's sword broke (9) .... the fight. Merlin arrived and said, 'Stop fighting, Pellinore. This knight is (10) .... King Arthur!'

0.	**A** at	**B** of	**C** on	**D** by
1.	**A** between	**B** among	**C** against	**D** again
2.	**A** all	**B** other	**C** some	**D** every
3.	**A** listen	**B** submit	**C** follow	**D** obey
4.	**A** for	**B** to	**C** at	**D** in
5.	**A** ride	**B** riding	**C** rode	**D** rides
6.	**A** a	**B** the	**C** one	**D** some
7.	**A** the	**B** one	**C** this	**D** a
8.	**A** them	**B** their	**C** they	**D** there
9.	**A** during	**B** while	**C** at	**D** on
10.	**A** his	**B** the	**C** you	**D** your

A Find the four hidden words that describe King Arthur. Circle them.

```
X K H E L D I C S J Y F M
O T U L W C E O H L J R C
P A D V E N T U R O U S N
S E G R A B H R O Y C P G
G R P L O Y E A T A U H I
A M L V K E U G P L B C B
B D J A F R I E N D L Y A
S C K X O S K O V H R O S
N Z V K P A J U X V A U H
P Q A J M I F S O Y F I T
Z I F B U N D B F M Y R X
```

B Now match the four hidden words with their meanings.

A person who...

a. makes many friends is ....
b. is not afraid is ....
c. you can trust is ....
d. likes doing exciting things is ....

 **Like + -ing**

The verb 'like' is followed by the gerund. Look at this sentence:
'He *liked* rid*ing* his horse and look*ing* for adventures.'

Fill in the gaps with the correct verbs from the box.

> liked fighting   didn't like riding
> liked causing trouble   didn't like living   likes reading
> doesn't like eating

a. He is never hungry. He ....
b. Sir Pellinore and Arthur fought with their swords. They ....
c. The noblemen did not obey Arthur. They ....
d. The Archbishop was afraid of horses. He ....
e. She read a book about King Arthur. She ....
f. The first Roman invaders did not stay in Britain. They .... there.

PET

 Imagine you are Arthur. You want to write a card to Sir Ector. In your card you should tell him about

- your difficulties at Camelot
- your ride in the forest
- your meeting with Sir Pellinore and what happened

Write 35-45 words.

Knights

The Knight was an important figure in the feudal system of the Middle Ages. A knight was a warrior.[1] He defended his king, his country and his church. He was a strong, courageous figure. He protected women, children, the poor and the weak. He fought for justice. He was generous with everyone. This was the Code of Chivalry, which he obeyed. Knights usually came from rich and noble families. They started their training when they were very young, as pages. Then they became squires and finally knights. It was a great honour to become a knight. Knights formed a separate social class in their kingdom.

Knights wore fine clothes. Their armour was heavy. Even their horses wore heavy armour. When a knight fought, he usually carried a shield,[2] a lance, a long sword, a battle-axe[3] and a knife. Each knight had a shield with a particular colour and design on it.

Jousting, a calendar scene for June from *The Golf Book* (1520-1530) by the workshop of Simon Bening.

1. **warrior** : champion fighter.
2. **shield** :
3. **battle-axe** :

Page

Age: from age 7 to the teen years
Duties: He learned to
- serve and obey his superiors
- ride a horse
- use weapons
- play special games
- hunt with falcons and hawks [1]

Squire

Age: from the teen years to 21 years old
Duties: He learned to
- fight in battle
- serve his lord
- assist his knight during a battle
- play Quintain, a battle sport

Knight

Age: 21 years old

During an important ceremony, the squire was dressed in red and black. Here he received knighthood. He promised to obey the Code of Chivalry. Now he was a knight and he served his king, queen or lord.

---

1. **falcons and hawks**: birds of prey.

The knight's armour and weapons

1 Complete the boxes.

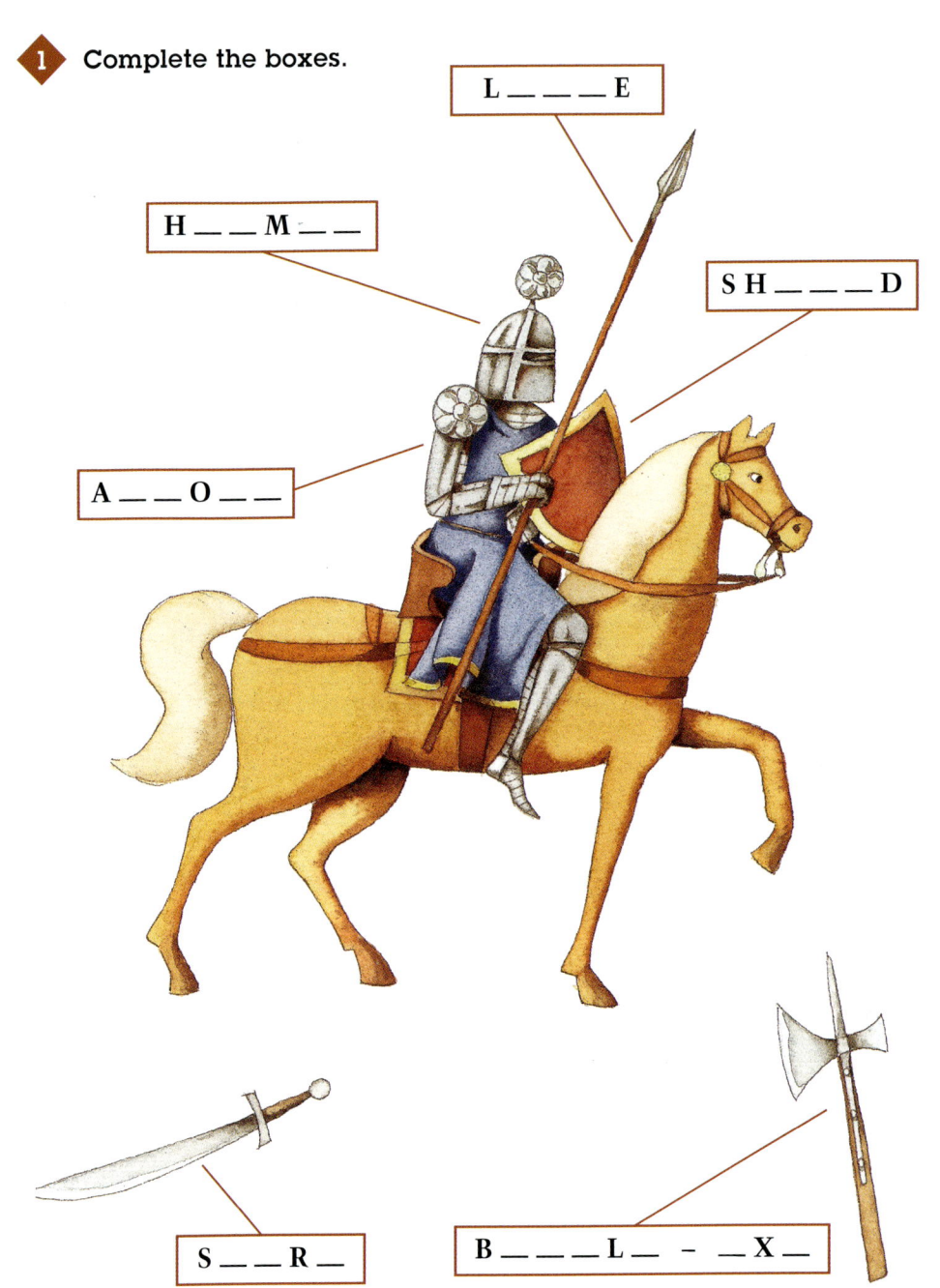

L _ _ _ E

H _ _ M _ _

S H _ _ _ _ D

A _ _ O _ _

S _ _ R _

B _ _ _ L _ - _ X _

CHAPTER FOUR

EXCALIBUR

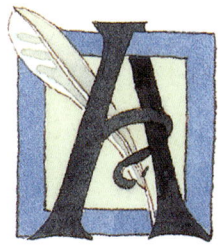rthur rode away with Merlin and said, 'I broke my sword during the fight with Sir Pellinore. I am king because of that sword. I must have another sword.'

'Come with me then,' said Merlin.

Arthur followed Merlin to a lake of clear water. In the middle of the lake, Arthur saw an arm. The arm was holding a sword in a beautiful scabbard.[1]

'Look!' said Merlin. 'That is the sword and that is the Lady of the Lake. Ask her kindly and the sword is yours.'

Arthur saw a beautiful lady in a boat on the lake. He asked her, 'Can I have that sword?'

---

1. **scabbard** : attached to your belt, where you keep a sword.

 # King Arthur
and his Knights

She answered, 'Yes, you can have it. Take my boat and go and get it.'

Arthur and Merlin went to the middle of the lake. There Arthur took the sword. He was very interested in it. He took the sword out of the scabbard and looked at it. It was a beautiful sword with jewels on it.

'Look, Merlin,' he said, 'the word Excalibur is written on it.'

'Yes, Excalibur is the greatest sword in the world. But its scabbard is more precious.'

'Why?' asked Arthur.

'It has a great magic power,' said Merlin. 'When you wear it, you never bleed [1] even if you are wounded. [2] When you fight, you must always have the scabbard with you.'

1. **bleed** : lose blood, the red liquid that runs in the body.
2. **wounded** : injured.

UNDERSTANDING THE TEXT

PET

1 Look at the statements below about Chapter Four.
Decide if each statement is correct or incorrect.
If it is correct, tick (✓) A.
If it is not correct, tick (✓) B.

                                                                                                                            A B

1. Arthur lost his sword during a fight with Sir Pellinore.
2. Merlin took Arthur to a forest.
3. Arthur saw an arm holding a sword in the middle of the lake.
4. Arthur asked the Lady of the Lake, 'May I have the sword?'
5. Arthur and Merlin swam to the middle of the lake and took the sword.
6. The sword had jewels on it.
7. The word 'king' was written on the sword.
8. The name of the sword was Excalibur.
9. The sword was more precious than the scabbard.
10. Merlin said, 'You will never bleed when you wear the scabbard.'

2 Prepositions
Fill in the blank spaces with the correct prepositions in the box.

        with (x2)   out   of   on   in   during

a. Arthur rode away .... Merlin.
b. Arthur broke his sword .... the fight with Sir Pellinore.
c. In the middle .... the lake, Arthur saw an arm holding a sword .... a beautiful scabbard.
d. He took the sword .... of the scabbard.
e. There was a word .... the sword.
f. When you fight, you must always keep the scabbard .... you.

CHAPTER FIVE

ARTHUR MEETS GUINEVERE

 A lot of enemies tried to invade Britain: the Saxons, the Jutes, the Pitts and others.
A big army of Saxons attacked King Leodegrance in his castle. He was the King of Cameliard. Young King Arthur and his knights fought against these Saxons and won.

King Leodegrance was very thankful [1] to Arthur. He invited him and his knights to a royal banquet. At the banquet, Arthur met the King's daughter, Princess

---

1. **thankful** : grateful, obliged.

KING ARTHUR
and his KNIGHTS

Guinevere. Guinevere was young and very beautiful. Arthur fell in love with her. He wanted to marry her.

Merlin wasn't happy with Arthur's choice,[1] but he accepted his king's decision.

King Leodegrance, Guinevere's father, was very happy about this marriage. 'I am honoured to give my daughter to our courageous king!' said Guinevere's father. 'My gift to King Arthur is the Round Table, which belonged to his father, King Uther.'

Arthur and Guinevere were married. There was an enormous banquet. Everyone in the kingdom was happy.

Guinevere arrived at King Arthur's castle with her ladies and the Round Table. The enormous Round Table had places for 150 knights. Arthur called the best knights of Britain to sit at the Round Table. Only the bravest knights were part of Arthur's court.

---

1. **choice** : preference, selection.

UNDERSTANDING THE TEXT

 Read the statements below.
For each statement, choose the correct answer – A, B, C or D.

1. The Saxons, Jutes and Pitts were
   - A ☐ tribes of southern Britain.
   - B ☐ enemies of Britain.
   - C ☐ King Arthur's friends.
   - D ☐ King Leodegrance's friends.

2. King Arthur fought against the Saxons and
   - A ☐ he lost the battle.
   - B ☐ he made peace with them.
   - C ☐ he won the battle.
   - D ☐ he was wounded.

3. King Leodegrance invited Arthur to a banquet
   - A ☐ but Arthur did not go.
   - B ☐ and Arthur met Princess Guinevere.
   - C ☐ and Arthur met the King's family.
   - D ☐ but Arthur did not like the food.

4. Arthur and Guinevere
   - A ☐ sat together at the banquet.
   - B ☐ became good friends.
   - C ☐ were married.
   - D ☐ did not speak the same language.

5. The Round Table was a gift
   - A ☐ from King Uther.
   - B ☐ from the Saxons.
   - C ☐ from Merlin.
   - D ☐ from King Leodegrance.

6. Arthur called the bravest knights of Britain
   - A ☐ to build the Round Table.
   - B ☐ to build a new castle.
   - C ☐ to sit at the Round Table.
   - D ☐ to fight against the Saxons.

2. Object pronouns

Look at these sentences from Chapter Five:

He invited *him* and his knights to a royal banquet.
***him* refers to Arthur**
Arthur fell in love with *her*.
***her* refers to Guinevere**

There are two types of pronouns, subject pronouns (*I, you, he, she, it, we, they*) and object pronouns (*me, you, him, her, it, us, them*). We use object pronouns as the direct or indirect object of a verb.

Choose the correct object pronouns and write them above the words in italics.

Look at this example:

Britain was in danger. A lot of enemies wanted to invade *Britain*. → it

a. A big army of Saxons attacked *King Leodegrance*.

b. Arthur helped King Leodegrance. King Leodegrance was thankful to *Arthur*.

c. King Leodegrance invited *Arthur and his knights* to a royal banquet.

d. King Leodegrance had a beautiful daughter. Arthur met *Princess Guinevere* at the banquet.

e. Merlin wasn't happy with Arthur's choice, but he accepted *his King's* decision.

f. King Leodegrance said, 'Thank you for protecting *me and my people*.'

g. The Round Table had places for 150 knights. Arthur called *the knights* to sit at the Round Table.

3. Crossword puzzle

ACROSS

1. The Round ....
2. Arthur's sword.
3. These enemies wanted to invade Britain.
4. The opposite of 'no'.
5. Arthur's real father.
6. Wise magician.

DOWN

1. The knights were very ....
2. King Arthur lived here.
3. King Arthur's wife.
4. A big group of soldiers.

BEFORE YOU READ

PET

1 **Listen to Chapter Six.**
For each question, put a tick (✓) in the correct box.

1. Five kings joined together because
   - A ☐ they wanted to conquer Denmark.
   - B ☐ they wanted to travel to Ireland.
   - C ☐ they wanted to conquer Britain.

2. King Arthur asked Guinevere
   - A ☐ to go with him and his knights.
   - B ☐ to stay in Camelot.
   - C ☐ to go to her father.

3. The five kings attacked
   - A ☐ in the early morning.
   - B ☐ during the night.
   - C ☐ at midday.

4. King Arthur, Guinevere and the knights
   - A ☐ were afraid.
   - B ☐ returned to Camelot.
   - C ☐ crossed the river and went to the forest.

5. In the moonlight they saw the five kings
   - A ☐ riding towards them.
   - B ☐ going away.
   - C ☐ eating dinner.

6. King Arthur and his knights
   - A ☐ made peace with the kings.
   - B ☐ killed the five kings.
   - C ☐ killed one of the kings.

CHAPTER SIX

THE FIVE KINGS

King Arthur and Queen Guinevere were very happy together. The people loved their beautiful queen.

Not long after their marriage, there was another invasion of Britain. The King of Ireland, the King of Denmark, and three other kings joined together. They wanted to conquer Britain with their strong armies.

'We must fight these five kings,' said King Arthur. 'We must protect Britain.'

The knights of the Round Table were ready to fight against the enemy.

Before leaving Camelot, Arthur said to Guinevere, 'Dear Guinevere, I don't want to leave you alone. Please come

KING ARTHUR
and his KNIGHTS

with me. I promise to protect you. Your lovely presence gives me happiness and courage.'

Guinevere smiled and said, 'Arthur, I am happy to follow you.'

Queen Guinevere rode next to King Arthur. King Arthur's army followed. After travelling for many days they did not meet the five kings.

Suddenly one night, the five kings attacked King Arthur's camp. They almost [1] destroyed the camp. The noise of the battle woke up King Arthur. He, Guinevere, and the other knights rode away quickly. They crossed the River Humber and went to the forest. Then they heard horses across the river. In the moonlight, they saw the five kings. The kings were riding towards them, and they were alone.

One knight said, 'Let's attack them by surprise! They're alone! They can't see us, but we can see them!'

King Arthur and his knights killed the five kings.

The enemy armies were confused without their leaders. They all left Britain. King Arthur and his knights were again victorious. They saved Britain from a dangerous invasion.

1. **almost** : nearly, practically.

UNDERSTANDING THE TEXT

PET

1 Look at the statements below about Chapter Six.
Decide if each statement is correct or incorrect.
If it is correct, tick (✓) A.
If it is not correct, tick (✓) B.

	A	B
1. The people of Camelot loved Queen Guinevere.	☐	☐
2. Soon after King Arthur's marriage, five kings wanted to conquer Britain.	☐	☐
3. The five kings came from Ireland.	☐	☐
4. The knights of the Round Table did not want to fight against the five kings.	☐	☐
5. When King Arthur went to fight against the enemy, Guinevere stayed in Camelot.	☐	☐
6. King Arthur went to fight against the five kings alone.	☐	☐
7. One night the five kings attacked King Arthur's camp.	☐	☐
8. King Arthur and his army attacked the five kings by surprise and killed them.	☐	☐
9. The enemy armies stayed in Britain.	☐	☐

2 Word puzzle

Read the definitions and write the words.

a. very pretty, lovely: B _ _ _ _ _ F _ _
b. male ruler of a country: _ _ _ G
c. opposite of weak: S _ _ _ _ G
d. take care of: P _ _ _ _ C _
e. there are many trees here: _ O _ _ S _
f. wife of a king: _ U _ _ _
g. not safe: D _ _ G _ _ _ _ S

43

Possessive adjectives

Look at these sentences:

The people loved *their* beautiful Queen.
Not long after *their* marriage, there was another invasion of Britain.

***Their* is a possessive adjective. The other possessive adjectives are:** *my, your, his, her, its, our.*

Fill in the gaps in the sentences below with the correct possessive adjectives.

a. Queen Guinevere rode .... brown horse.

b. 'This is .... fountain!' said Sir Pellinore.

c. 'The five kings attacked .... camp!' said the knights.

d. Merlin wasn't happy with Arthur's choice, but he accepted .... King's decision.

e. 'Excalibur is .... new sword,' said Merlin to Arthur.

f. The noblemen did not obey .... King.

T: GRADE 5

 Topic – Transport
In this chapter, the knights rode their horses to go to fight the enemy.
Have you ever ridden a horse?
Bring a picture or a photo of a means of transport in your country. Tell the class about it using these questions to help you.

a. Is it a popular means of transport? Who uses it?

b. How do you travel to school?

c. What other means of transport have you ever used, either in your country or elsewhere? Have you ever used any unusual type of transport?

d. Are there any problems with public transport in your country?

CHAPTER SEVEN

LANCELOT

ne of the knights of the Round Table was Lancelot. He came from France. Lancelot was very kind and generous. He often gave his things [1] to the poor.

Lancelot served his king and queen well. One day a strange girl came to the great hall of the castle. She said to Sir Lancelot, 'Come with me! It's very important. I cannot tell you more. Please follow me.'

Sir Lancelot followed the girl to the forest. They stopped at a church.

Lancelot entered the church. He saw twelve nuns. [2] One

1. **things** : possessions.
2. **nuns** :

 # King Arthur
and his Knights

nun said, 'Sir Lancelot, we bring you this young man. He is loyal and courageous. Please make him a knight.'

The young man looked honest. Lancelot agreed to make him a knight. However, Lancelot did not recognize this young man. He was the son Lancelot had from Elaine, a lady he loved some years before. The young man's name was Galahad. Galahad's mother wanted him to be a knight, like his father.

The next day, Lancelot returned to Camelot with the young knight. King Arthur, Queen Guinevere and the knights of the Round Table were happy to meet Galahad.

When Sir Galahad sat down at the Round Table, his name appeared on the table! Everyone was amazed.[1] Lancelot looked at Galahad carefully. Suddenly, he realised that Galahad was his son! Lancelot was very happy and proud.[2]

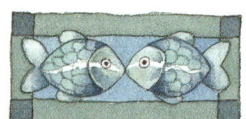

1. **amazed** : very surprised.
2. **proud** : satisfied, pleased.

UNDERSTANDING THE TEXT

PET

Read the statements below.
For each statement choose the correct answer – A, B, C or D.

1. Lancelot came from
   - A ☐ London.
   - B ☐ Ireland.
   - C ☐ Denmark.
   - D ☐ France.

2. He followed a strange girl to
   - A ☐ a castle.
   - B ☐ a forest.
   - C ☐ a river.
   - D ☐ a town.

3. A nun in a church said to Lancelot,
   - A ☐ 'Please make this man a knight.'
   - B ☐ 'Please take this man to Camelot.'
   - C ☐ 'Please give this man a magic sword.'
   - D ☐ 'Please take this man to the lake.'

4. The young man was Lancelot's
   - A ☐ enemy.
   - B ☐ brother.
   - C ☐ friend.
   - D ☐ son.

5. Elaine was Galahad's
   - A ☐ wife.
   - B ☐ sister.
   - C ☐ mother.
   - D ☐ friend.

6. When Galahad sat down at the Round Table his name appeared
   - A ☐ on the table.
   - B ☐ on the wall.
   - C ☐ on the chair.
   - D ☐ on his sword.

2 **A** Which adjectives or nouns describe these characters? Some can be used more than once. Choose the words from the box.

Merlin	
Arthur	
Lancelot	
Guinevere	
Galahad	

> wife   counsellor   beautiful   wise   king   friendly
> courageous   generous   magician   queen   kind
> loyal   adventurous   knight

B Now make sentences that describe these characters.

a. Merlin is a .... He is ....

b. Arthur is a .... He is ....

c. Lancelot is a .... He is ....

d. Guinevere is a .... She is ....

e. Galahad is a .... He is ....

3. The imperative

The imperative in English is the same as the infinitive of the verb, without 'to'.
In Chapter Seven, we saw these imperative sentences:

Come with me!
Please follow me!
Please make him a knight.

To form a negative imperative, we add 'do not', 'don't' or 'never' before the verb:

Don't follow me!
Never go to the forest alone!

Complete the following sentences with the imperatives in the box.

don't open	look at	do not enter	give money
stop	take me	follow me	tell me

a. The girl wants Sir Lancelot to go with her. She says, '……………………!'

b. Lancelot must not enter the church. The nun says, '…………………… this church!'

c. Lancelot often gave his things to the poor. He told his friends, '…………………… to the poor!'

d. Galahad wanted to see King Arthur. He told Lancelot, '…………………… to him!'

e. It's very cold outside. '…………………… the door!'

f. Guinevere wants to know Arthur's story. She asks him, '…………………… your story!'

g. Merlin said to Sir Pellinore, '…………………… fighting!'

h. Sir Galahad sees his name on the Round Table. '…………………… the table!' he tells everyone.

Castles

Long ago castles were built to protect people from enemies. The first castles were made of wood. They were small and were built on hills. There was a high fence [1] all around them. Families lived in huts, [2] in the field [3] below. When the enemy attacked, they all ran to the castle.

With time, castles were made of rocks. [4] They were much stronger and bigger than the first castles. They had very thick walls. It was difficult for the enemy to attack this type of castle. Castles were

Capture of Wark Castle from the *Croniques de France et d'Angleterre* (1460-1480) by Jean Frossart.

1. **fence** : (here) a division made of stone or wood.
2. **huts** : very small houses.
3. **field** : flat land.
4. **rocks** : big stones.

built to protect important places. They were built on mountains and near rivers and seas.

There are many old castles in the world today. Many are open to the public. It is interesting to visit old castles and see how people lived in the past.

Every castle had a dungeon. It was a cold, dark place for prisoners. Many people lived and worked in a castle. There were noblemen with their families, warriors, servants, jesters[1] and musicians. It was like a village.

1 How much do you remember?

ACROSS

1. Members of the nobility.
2. Soldiers who attacked the castle.
3. A cold, dark place.
4. People who made music in the castle.
5. Where ordinary people lived.

DOWN

6. Flat land.
7. High area where castles were built.
8. A person who makes people laugh.
9. A division.

---

1. **jesters** : in the Middle Ages these men made the people at the castle laugh.

Banquet scene from *Les Très Riches Heures du Duc de Berry* (early 15th century) by the Limbourg brothers.

Old Castles of Great Interest

1. Bamburgh Castle was built in the 6th century in Northumberland. It was built on a high cliff. It is surrounded on three sides by the sea. Many films were made here.

2. Carlisle Castle was built at the end of the 11th century by William Rufus. It is near Scotland. At first, it was a wooden castle. In 1122, Henry I built walls of stone.

3. Dover Castle was originally a fort, built by the Celts. Then the Romans built a lighthouse,[1] which you can still visit. Later, Bishop Odo of Bayeux built the great Dover Castle.

4. Edinburgh Castle was built in Edinburgh, Scotland. In the 7th century, King Edwin built a fortress on a big rock. Later, it became a great castle.

1. **lighthouse** : a tower containing a powerful lamp, used to guide ships.

Put the name of each castle below its description.

a. The Romans built a lighthouse here.
　　..

b. It is surrounded by the sea on three sides.
　　..

c. King Edwin built it in the 7th century in Scotland.
　　..

d. It was a wooden castle at first.
　　..

Which of these four castles do you like best? Why?

Project on the Web

▶▶ Let's find out some more information about the places where King Arthur was born, where he lived and where he fought. Your teacher will help you to find the correct Web site.

Discover how these places are related to King Arthur. Write a few sentences about each one.
- Tintagel
- Cadbury Castle
- Glastonbury
- Winchester

Can you find any other places related to King Arthur? Tell the class about the information you found.
Now look again at the map on page 5 to see where these places are situated. You can add any new places you found onto this map.

BEFORE YOU READ

1 Listen to Chapter Eight and look at the six sentences below.
Decide if each sentence is correct or incorrect.
If it is correct, put a tick (✓) in the box under A for YES.
If it is not correct, put a tick (✓) in the box under B for NO.

	A	B
1. Sir Gawain carried a green bowl around the room.	☐	☐
2. King Arthur recognized the Holy Grail.	☐	☐
3. The knights were not interested in the Holy Grail.	☐	☐
4. The search for the Holy Grail was dangerous.	☐	☐
5. Galahad, Percival and Bors found the Holy Grail.	☐	☐
6. After finding the Holy Grail, Galahad returned to Camelot and told everyone about his experience.	☐	☐

CHAPTER EIGHT

THE HOLY GRAIL

ne day the knights were sitting at the Round Table. They were celebrating a religious holiday. Suddenly, there was a loud noise. Then there was a strong light.

A green bowl [1] covered with a cloth moved around the room. Invisible hands carried it. After a few moments, the green bowl disappeared.

'That was the Holy Grail!' exclaimed King Arthur. 'That is where Christ's blood was kept after he was crucified.'

The knights were amazed. They all wanted to see the Holy Grail.

1. bowl :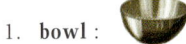

King Arthur
and his Knights

Sir Gawain, a loyal knight, declared, 'I want to look for the Grail for one year and one day.'

'Yes, I want to look for the Grail too,' said another knight.

All the knights wanted to travel to distant lands to find the Holy Grail. There was great excitement at the Round Table.

King Arthur was very worried. He knew that the search [1] for the Holy Grail was dangerous. In fact, many knights died during the search. Others never returned to Camelot.

Only three knights found the Holy Grail. They were Galahad, Percival and Bors. All three had pure hearts. Only those with pure hearts saw the Holy Grail. The three knights travelled to distant lands. After many dangerous adventures, they found the Holy Grail.

When they saw it on a silver table, they thanked God for this great happiness. After finding the Grail, Galahad and Percival died. But Bors returned to Camelot. He told everyone about his wonderful experience.

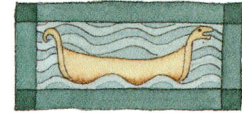

1. **search** : attempt to look for something.

UNDERSTANDING THE TEXT

PET

 Read the text below and choose the correct word for each space.
For each question, mark the letter next to the correct word – A, B, C or D.

The Knights (0) ...C... celebrating a religious holiday when they heard a loud noise. A green (1) .... covered (2) .... a cloth moved (3) .... the room. Then it disappeared. King Arthur said, 'That is (4) .... Christ's blood was kept after he was crucified.' All the knights were very surprised. Sir Gawain said, 'I want to look (5) .... the Holy Grail.' All the knights wanted to find it. King Arthur knew that the (6) .... for the Grail was dangerous. Many knights (7) .... returned to Camelot. Three knights (8) .... the Holy Grail. Only (9) .... with pure hearts could see it. Bors returned to Camelot and told (10) .... about his experience.

0.	A is	B be	C were	D was
1.	A bowl	B cup	C dish	D basin
2.	A at	B on	C by	D with
3.	A by	B around	C on	D at
4.	A where	B wear	C were	D in
5.	A by	B in	C for	D on
6.	A examination	B search	C research	D investigation
7.	A no	B not	C ever	D never
8.	A found	B finding	C find	D finds
9.	A this	B these	C those	D that
10.	A any	B anyone	C everyone	D every

2. Crack the code!

Can you discover what these words are?
Use the secret code, unscramble them, and you will find a question.

A = ♥   O = ♠   E = ✿
U = ❀   I = ✭

1. ✿ r h ✿ w =   _ _ _ _ _
2. s ✭ =   _ _
3. h ✿ t =   _ _ _
4. y ♠ h l =   _ _ _ _
5. l ♥ r ✭ g =   _ _ _ _ _
6. ♠ w n =   _ _ _ ?

Do you know the answer?

3. Imagine you are Sir Gawain.
You want to write a card to your mother and father.
In your card you should tell them

- about the Holy Grail
- why you want to travel to distant lands
- who will go with you

Write 35-45 words.

PET

 4 For each question, complete the second sentence so that it means the same as the first, <u>using no more than three words</u>.

    0. The town is called Black Castle.
        The ..name.of................. the town is Black Castle.

    1. The book ends with an exciting journey.
        There is an exciting journey .... of the book.

    2. There is danger in travelling in the forest at night.
        Travelling in the forest at night ....

    3. The King of Denmark is very unpopular.
        Nobody .... the King of Denmark.

    4. The battle lasted six hours.
        The battle was .... after six hours.

    5. The weight of the sword was three kilograms.
        The sword .... three kilograms.

T: GRADE 5

 5 **Topic – Festivals**
Before the Holy Grail appeared, the knights were celebrating a religious holiday.

Tell the class about a traditional celebration or festival you have taken part in. Bring in a photo or a picture of this celebration or festival and use these questions to help you.

    a. What is the celebration/festival?
    b. What are the origins of this celebration/festival?
    c. When did you take part in this celebration?
    d. How did everyone celebrate?
    e. Did you have a good time?

BEFORE YOU READ

PET

 Below are the notes of a historian at King Arthur's court.
Listen to Chapter Nine.
For each question, fill in the missing information in the numbered space.

NOTES FOR THE BATTLE AT DOVER

Year: 537

King Arthur leaves Britain

Sir Gawain and other (1) .... go with King Arthur to fight in a distant land.

King Arthur asks Mordred to (2) .... his land until his return.

Mordred

Mordred wants to become King of Britain. 'King Arthur was (3) .... in the war,' he tells everyone. And Mordred becomes king.

Dover

King Arthur is (4) .... and returns to Dover with his knights. The (5) .... at Dover is terrible and very long. Only King Arthur and (6) .... remain alive. Then King Arthur kills Mordred. Now the King is dying!

CHAPTER NINE

KING ARTHUR GOES TO AVALON

 King Arthur lived a long life, but it finished sadly. In the search for the Holy Grail, many of his knights left Britain. Other knights died. Arthur was alone.

In 537, King Arthur went to a distant land to fight. Sir Gawain and other loyal knights went with him. Before leaving Camelot, King Arthur spoke to a knight called Mordred. He said, 'Mordred, I ask you to rule[1] my land until I return. I know you are a loyal man.'

---

1. **rule** : govern.

King Arthur
and his Knights

King Arthur and his knights left Britain to go to war. But Mordred was not loyal. He wanted to take King Arthur's place. He wanted to be King of Britain!

So Mordred told everyone that Arthur was killed in the war, in France. Mordred became King of Britain! He was made King in Canterbury.

When King Arthur heard the news, he was furious. He returned to Britain immediately. He and his knights arrived in Dover. Here he found Mordred and his army. They were waiting for him.

There was a long, terrible battle. Only King Arthur and Sir Bedivere remained alive. Sir Gawain died in Arthur's arms. The King buried[1] him in Dover Castle.

Arthur fought a long battle against Mordred.

At the end of the battle, King Arthur took his spear[2] and killed Mordred. But Mordred's sword went through Arthur's helmet and his head.

The great king was dying! He still had to do one thing. He called Sir Bedivere and said, 'I must give my sword Excalibur back to the Lady of the Lake. Take it to the lake. Then throw it far into the water.'

Sir Bedivere went to the lake. He threw Excalibur far into the water. An arm came out of the water and caught the sword. Then it disappeared into the water.

---

1. **buried** : put in the ground.
2. **spear** : a type of lance.

KING ARTHUR
and his KNIGHTS

Sir Bedivere returned to King Arthur. He told him about what he saw at the lake. Arthur was satisfied and said, 'Thank you, my loyal friend. Now carry me to the lake.'

At the lake, there was a boat waiting for Arthur. The Lady of the Lake was in it.

'Put me in the boat,' said Arthur. Sir Bedivere obeyed and said, 'What can I do without you, my king?'

Arthur answered, 'My life is near the end. Pray [1] for yourself! Prayers can do many things. Farewell! [2] I am going to Avalon.' [3]

The boat moved away slowly. Sir Bedivere watched the boat on the lake until it disappeared.

1. **Pray** : speak to God, ask God for help.
2. **Farewell** : goodbye.
3. **Avalon** : the land of the dead in Celtic mythology.

UNDERSTANDING THE TEXT

 Look at the statements below about Chapter Nine.
Decide if each statement is correct or incorrect.
If it is correct, tick (✓) A.
If it is incorrect, tick (✓) B.

	A	B
1. In the search for the Holy Grail, many of the knights left Britain.	☐	☐
2. In 537 King Arthur went to a distant land to live.	☐	☐
3. Before leaving Camelot, King Arthur said to Mordred, 'Please rule my land until my return.'	☐	☐
4. Mordred told everyone that King Arthur was killed in France.	☐	☐
5. Mordred then became King of France.	☐	☐
6. King Arthur and his army returned and fought against Mordred.	☐	☐
7. At the end of the battle Mordred died and Arthur was wounded.	☐	☐
8. Sir Bedivere threw Excalibur into the forest.	☐	☐
9. Sir Bedivere carried the dying Arthur to the lake.	☐	☐
10. King Arthur said, 'Farewell! I am going to Camelot.'	☐	☐

 Look at the text in each question.
What does it say?
Mark the letter next to the correct explanation – A, B or C.

0.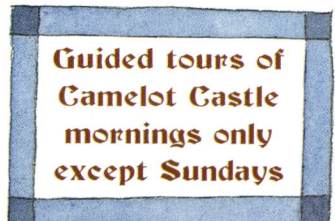

Guided tours of
Camelot Castle
mornings only
except Sundays

- A ☐ You can visit the castle at 10 a.m. on Sunday.
- B ☐ You can visit the castle only on Sundays.
- C ☑ You can visit the castle on Tuesday at 11 a.m.

1. *Swords not allowed inside the Church*

- A ☐ Leave your sword outside the church.
- B ☐ You can leave your sword at the back of the church.
- C ☐ Swords are not allowed near the church.

2. **Knights' Association weekly meeting cancelled**

- A ☐ The Knights' Association will meet at Christmas.
- B ☐ There is no meeting of the Knights' Association this week.
- C ☐ The Knights' Association meets at weekends.

3. Horses use other side of the road

- A ☐ Horses should walk on the other side of the road.
- B ☐ The road is dangerous for horses.
- C ☐ This road is for horses only.

4. from 20 February please use new castle entrance

- A ☐ The castle will be closed after 20 February.
- B ☐ This castle entrance is closed in February.
- C ☐ The new castle entrance will be open on 20 February.

3 **The contracted form or genitive 's?**

Sometimes we confuse the genitive 's' with the contracted form of the verbs *is* or *has*. Look at these examples:

Sir Gawain died in Arthur's arms.
Here the 's means the *arms of Arthur*.

Arthur's going to fight Sir Pellinore. **(Arthur is going to...)**
He's got a big sword. **(He has got...)**
Here the 's means *is* or *has*.

Change these sentences to the genitive 's', or to the contracted verb form.

a. The life of Arthur was long.
   ....

b. King Arthur is going to France.
   ....

c. The army of Mordred was in Dover.
   ....

d. Sir Bedivere has taken Excalibur to the lake.
   ....

Now decide if the 's is the *genitive* or *is* or *has*.

e. The lady's bringing the boat.
   ....

f. Galahad's looking for the Holy Grail.
   ....

g. Lancelot's got many friends.
   ....

h. The knight's trip was dangerous.
   ....

Summary of the story

Fill in the gaps with the words from the box, and you will have a summary of the book.

Holy Grail	Galahad	Bors	Excalibur	stone	noblemen
pulls	magician	king	the year	married	Merlin
great church	sword	good	new	Arthur	true	written
Christmas Day	Round Table	return	Percival	Archbishop
died	Mordred (x2)	army	Avalon	disappeared

In .... 509, Britain had no .... Merlin, the ...., went to the .... of Canterbury and said, 'We must have a king. Tell all the .... of the kingdom to meet at the .... in London on ....'

Outside the church there was a big .... with a .... in it. These words were .... on the stone:

'He who .... the sword out of this stone is the .... King of Britain.'

Young .... pulled the sword out of the stone. He was the .... King of Britain. Arthur was a .... king. His people loved him. One day Arthur and .... went to a lake. Here Arthur received his famous sword, ...

Arthur .... Princess Guinevere. As a wedding gift, King Leodegrance gave Arthur the .... Only the best knights sat at the Round Table.

One day the .... appeared to Arthur and his knights. Then it ....

Three knights wanted to look for it. They were ...., ... and .... Galahad found it, but then he died.

In 537, Arthur went to France to fight. He asked .... to rule the land until his .... But .... wanted to take Arthur's place! When Arthur heard this, he returned to Britain. Here Arthur fought against Mordred and his .... Both Arthur and Mordred .... Finally, the Lady of the Lake took Arthur to ....

The Round Table

What happened to King Arthur's Round Table? In the old castle in Winchester, there is an enormous round table. It is hanging on the wall. In 1485, William Caxton, the first English printer, said that this round table was King Arthur's.

The names of 24 knights are painted on the table. King Arthur's place has no name on it. Instead, his picture is painted on it. Some of the knights mentioned on the table are: Sir Lancelot, Sir Galahad, Sir Pellinore, Sir Gawain, Sir Bedivere, Sir Ector and Sir Mordred.

This is King Arthur's Round Table with 24 of his named Knights at Winchester Hall.

1 Who are they?
Match the description to the character(s).

a. He fought with King Arthur near a fountain.
b. They found the Holy Grail.
c. He pulled the sword out of the rock on New Year's Day.
d. He raised Arthur well.
e. He came from France.
f. She was King Leodegrance's daughter.
g. He took King Arthur's place as King of Britain.
h. King Arthur buried him in Dover Castle.
i. He carried dying King Arthur to the lake.
j. She was beautiful and lived by the lake.
k. He was a magician.
l. He was the King of Cameliard.

1. ☐ Lancelot
2. ☐ King Leodegrance
3. ☐ Sir Bedivere
4. ☐ Guinevere
5. ☐ Sir Gawain
6. ☐ Pellinore
7. ☐ Lady of the Lake
8. ☐ Galahad, Bors and Percival
9. ☐ Mordred
10. ☐ Merlin
11. ☐ Sir Ector
12. ☐ Arthur

Where was King Arthur Buried?

At the end of the 12th century, the monks of an abbey in Glastonbury discovered a grave. On the tombstone of this grave there were these Latin words:

Hic Jacet Arthurus Rex Quondam Rexque Futurus
(Here lies Arthur, once King and King to be)

Was this King Arthur's grave? Before dying, Arthur said to Bedivere, 'I am going to Avalon.'

The medieval remains of Glastonbury Abbey.

In a writing of the 12th century, the word Avalon meant [1] 'the island of apples.' The name Glastonbury came from the name of a peasant, [2] Glasteing. This peasant built a house near a big apple tree. Later, a church was built here. The name Glasteing became Glastonbury, near the River Severn. Today, Glastonbury is in the county of Somerset.

The Latin words, 'Rexque Futurus' mean that King Arthur will perhaps return one day, if his people need him!

1. **meant** : signified.
2. **peasant** : person who works on the land.

You want to tell your best friend about your visit to Glastonbury. Fill in the gaps and your letter will be ready.

Dear .... ,

Yesterday I visited King Arthur's ¹........................... in Glastonbury. It was very interesting. The ²........................... at the abbey discovered it in the ³........................... century.

The name Glastonbury comes from the name of a ⁴........................... called Glasteing. Glasteing built his ⁵........................... near an ⁶........................... tree.

A ⁷........................... was built there many years later. Before ⁸..........................., King Arthur said he was going to Avalon. In the 12th century, the word Avalon meant ⁹........................... of apples.

Glastonbury is ¹⁰........................... the River Severn, in the county of Somerset. Go and visit it one day!

Love from

....

EXIT TEST

 Read the statements below. For each statement choose the correct answer – A, B, C or D.

1. King Uther Pendragon's counsellor was
   A ☐ Sir Ector.
   B ☐ Merlin.
   C ☐ The Archbishop of Canterbury.
   D ☐ Mordred.

2. King Arthur's real father was
   A ☐ Sir Gawain.
   B ☐ Merlin.
   C ☐ Sir Ector.
   D ☐ King Uther.

3. Arthur's first years as king were
   A ☐ difficult.
   B ☐ fun.
   C ☐ exciting.
   D ☐ boring.

4. The Lady of the Lake gave
   A ☐ Merlin a sword.
   B ☐ Arthur the Round Table.
   C ☐ Arthur his sword, Excalibur.
   D ☐ Mordred a magic scabbard.

5. King Leodegrance was the King of
   A ☐ Camelot.
   B ☐ Cameliard.
   C ☐ Britain.
   D ☐ Avalon.

6. King Arthur met Guinevere
   A ☐ in the forest.
   B ☐ on the lake.
   C ☐ at Camelot.
   D ☐ at a royal banquet.

7. Lancelot was
   - A ☐ Guinevere's brother.
   - B ☐ a knight from France.
   - C ☐ King Leodegrance's son.
   - D ☐ King Arthur's brother.

8. Many knights travelled to distant lands
   - A ☐ to look for adventures.
   - B ☐ to find new lands.
   - C ☐ to look for a magic sword.
   - D ☐ to look for the Holy Grail.

9. King Arthur thought that Mordred was
   - A ☐ strong.
   - B ☐ clever.
   - C ☐ loyal.
   - D ☐ rich.

10. Mordred told everyone that
    - A ☐ King Arthur was killed in battle.
    - B ☐ King Arthur wanted to stay in France.
    - C ☐ King Arthur went to Avalon.
    - D ☐ King Arthur was very ill.

11. After a long battle in Dover
    - A ☐ King Arthur was wounded and Mordred escaped.
    - B ☐ King Arthur was wounded and Mordred died.
    - C ☐ King Arthur and Mordred went to France.
    - D ☐ King Arthur and Mordred went to Camelot.

12. Sir Bedivere took Excalibur
    - A ☐ to Camelot.
    - B ☐ to the forest.
    - C ☐ to the boat.
    - D ☐ to the lake.

Score

2 Put the verbs in brackets into the Past Simple tense.

When Arthur (1) .... (be) born, Merlin (2) ....
(give) him to Sir Ector and his wife. They (3) .... (love) him
like a son. After King Uther's death, Britain (4) .... (have)
no king. There (5) .... (be) lots of problems.
On Christmas Day, outside the big church in Canterbury, the
noblemen (6) .... (see) a big stone with a sword in it. Only
the true King of Britain (7) .... (can) pull the sword out of
the stone.
Many noblemen (8) .... (try) to pull the sword out of the
stone. Young Arthur (9) .... (pull) it out without any
difficulty. On that day he (10) .... (become) the new King
of Britain. He was a courageous king and (11) .... (fight)
against enemies from other lands. Unfortunately he was wounded
by Mordred and he (12) .... (die).

3 Let's describe them!
Look at the adjectives in the box below. Use them to complete the
sentences about the characters in the story.

> brave   generous   young   magic
> loyal   beautiful   pure

a. Guinevere was .... and ....
b. Merlin had .... powers.
c. Mordred was not .... to his king.
d. Sir Lancelot was .... with the poor.
e. Galahad had a .... heart.
f. Only very .... knights could sit at the Round Table.

KEY TO THE EXIT TEST

1 1. B / 2. D / 3. A / 4. C / 5. B / 6. D / 7. B / 8. D / 9. C / 10. A / 11. B / 12. D

2 1. was 2. gave 3. loved 4. had 5. were 6. saw 7. could 8. tried 9. pulled 10. became 11. fought 12. died

3 a. young ... beautiful b. magic c. loyal d. generous e. pure f. brave